Buford Family Favorites

Copyright ©2021 by Al G. Buford

Welcome

This book is dedicated to the memory of my Grandmother and my mother Richella King Vinson (Big Momma), and Pollie Ann Vinson Buford from whom I acquired my love for cooking. Both were parents of ten children, I'm Pollie's 8th child and youngest of 6 sons. Thank you to my entire family for all of your love and support. I am so grateful for you all. A special shout out to those that contributed to the book with recipes: my sisters Linda Barrett and Carolyn Buford, my brother, Raymond Buford, and my beautiful daughter, Lisha Shaffer. A special thanks to my daughter, Regina Buford, for helping me put this, my first cook book on paper. And a very special shout out to my wife, Toni Buford, for her love and support throughout this entire process.

TABLE OF CONTENTS

GRILLED LEMON CHICKEN

Ingredients

2 Skinless, Boneless, Chicken Breasts (trim off fat)

½ cp Freshly Squeezed Lemon Juice

2 Large Cloves of Garlic, Minced

1 tbsp Fresh Oregano, Chopped

1 tsp Fresh Ginger, Minced

½ tsp Tomato Paste

1 Jalapeno Pepper, Seeded and Finely Chopped (optional)

Freshly Ground Pepper to Taste

Directions

In a large bowl, combine the lemon juice, garlic, oregano, ginger, tomato paste and jalapeno. Seasoned with ground pepper to taste. Add the chicken to the marinade and be sure to coat well. Place chicken breast with marinade into sealed plastic bags and refrigerate for 2 to 6 hours. Prepare the grill drain the chicken and discard the marinade. Grill the chicken until no longer pink inside (about 5 to 6 minutes each side)

MULTI- PURPOSE MARINADE

Ingredients

1 cp Soy Sauce

¼ cp Lemon Juice

1 cp Orange Juice

1 cp Pineapple Juice

½ cp Light Brown Sugar

1 tbsp Granulated Garlic

1 tbsp Onion Powder

Water to Cover Items

POTATO SALAD

Ingredients

3lbs Red Potatoes (Peeled and Medium Diced)

2 tsp Salt

1 cp Sweet Pickle Relish

6 Boiled Eggs (5 Diced And 1 Sliced)

1½ cp Miracle Whip Salad Dressing

2 tbsp Prepared Yellow Mustard

½ cp Chopped Celery

½ tsp Ground Black Pepper

Directions

Place potatoes in a medium saucepan and cover with cold water, bring to a boil. Reduce heat and cook just until potatoes are fork tender, do not overcook. Immediately shock potatoes with cold water and cool completely. Drain and transfer potatoes to a large mixing bowl, add remaining ingredients one at a time, mixing well after each addition. Garnish with the sliced hard boiled eggs, and Paprika. Cover and refrigerate. Serve cold. For smaller batches, reduce quantities.

FRIED APPLES

Ingredients

2 apples

½ cp Brown Sugar

1 tsp Corn Starch

½ cp Pecans

¾ cp water

½ tsp cinnamon

3 tbsp Butter

Directions

In frying pan melt butter, sauté apples, add water, combine dry ingredients, and add to pan. Simmer until done

CRAB CAKES

Ingredients

3 – 6oz cans Crab Meat (Drain and Squeeze Dry, But Retain the Liquid)

½ cp Contadina Traditional Breadcrumbs

1tsp Ground Ginger

2tsp Onion Powder

1tsp Granulated Garlic

1tsp Old Bay Seasoning

½ tsp Cumin

1½ tsp Paprika

2 Eggs (Beaten)

½ cp Reserved Liquid

Directions

Place crab meat into a large mixing bowl, add all dry ingredients, mix in eggs and liquid, shape into patties, coat with bread crumbs and fry in hot olive oil until golden brown.

COLE SLAW

Ingredients

1lb Thinly Shredded Green Cabbage

½lb Shaved Carrots

1tbsp White Vinegar

¼tsp Ground Black Pepper

1tsp Granulated Garlic

2tsp Granulated Sugar

1 ½ cp Miracle Whip Salad Dressing

Directions

Combine all ingredients, mix well and refrigerate 30 minutes. Serve cold for best results.

Cole Slaw; see Page 8

TUNA SALAD

Ingredients

2 Cans Tuna

2 Hard Boiled Eggs, Chopped

½ Cup Pickle Relish

½ Cup Miracle Whip

1 tbsp Sugar

1 tsp Prepared Mustard

Directions

Drain tuna and remove as much liquid as possible. Add remaining ingredients and mix well. Chill and serve cold

Variations

Substitute chicken or turkey for the tuna

Add one cup cooked macaroni

CANDIED YAMS

Ingredients

2lbs Yams or Sweet Potatoes

1cp Light Brown Sugar

¾ cp Granulated Sugar

½ tsp Cinnamon

¾ tsp Nutmeg

3 tbsp Corn Starch

½ tsp Vanilla

Directions

Peel and slice potatoes. Place in a medium sauce pan and add cold water just to cover potatoes. Bring to a boil, reduce heat and cook just until ¾'s done. In a small bowl, combine all dry ingredients and blend with a fork. Pour mixture over potatoes, add vanilla and continue to cook just until fork tender, do not overcook. Serve hot. For smaller batches, reduce quantities.

FRESH TOMATO PATCH SALAD

Ingredients

1 Cucumber, Chopped

1 Zucchini, Chopped

3 Ripe Roma Tomatoes, Chopped

¼ cp Red Onions, Chopped

2 tbsp Wine Vinegar

1tsp Salt

Fresh Ground Pepper

2 tbsp Fresh Mint Leaves, Chopped

2 tbsp Fresh Basil, Chopped

Directions

1. Peel, seed and chop the Cucumber and Zucchini. Combine Cucumbers and Zucchini with one tsp of salt in 2 tbsp of vinegar. Set aside for 30 minutes to extract the moisture from the Cucumbers.
2. Drain the Cucumbers and Zucchini, rinse under cold water and then toss with chopped Tomatoes and Red Onions.
3. Add a bit of Olive Oil to taste, season with freshly ground pepper.
4. Toss with Mint and Basil

CORN MEAL BREADING MIX

Ingredients

1cp Yellow Corn Meal

1tbsp plus 1 ½ tsp Lawry's Seasoned Salt

2tbsp Paprika

1 tsp Granulated Garlic

1 tsp Onion Powder

¼ tsp Ground Black Pepper

¼ cup All purpose Flour

Great for meats and vegetables

Dip in egg wash, then in breading mix and lay on foil lined pan

For oven fried, brush with Olive Oil and bake 20-25 minutes, until brown. For thicker breading, double dip. For larger batches, increase quantities.

Oven Fried Catfish; use Corn Meal Breading Mix, Page 12

CRACKLIN BREAD

Ingredients

10oz Yellow Corn Meal

10oz All Purpose Flour

3oz Granulate Sugar

1oz Baking Powder

1½ oz Non-Fat Dry Milk

2tsp Salt

4 Eggs

17oz Water (2 1/8 cp)

1oz Corn Syrup (2 tbsp)

6oz Melted Butter

2cp Crackling

Directions

Mix all dry ingredients together in a large mixing bowl, add water, syrup and butter. In a separate bowl, beat eggs well and then fold into mixture, add crackling and let mixture sit for 20 to 30 minutes. Spray pan with Mazola Pure Cooking Spray, add mixture and bake in a 425-degree pre heated oven for 25 minutes or until brown

SAVORY SMOTHERED POTATOES

Ingredients

2 lb White Potatoes

1-3 Green Onion Bulbs

½ tsp White Pepper

1tsp Garlic

1 tbsp Lawry's Seasoned Salt

1 tbsp Lemon Juice

1 ½ cp Water

Directions

Peel and slice potatoes in ¼ slices, set aside in cold water and lemon juice. In a large Skillet heat olive oil over medium-high heat. Add onion and garlic. Sauté for 2 minutes. Add water and potatoes, simmer until done

DEEP FRYING BATTER

Ingredients

¼ cp Corn Starch

1 tsp Lawry's Seasoned Salt

¼ tsp Black Pepper

¼ tsp Granulated Garlic

¼ tsp Onion Powder

1 cp Cold Milk

Breadcrumbs

Directions

Combine all ingredients, except breadcrumbs. Blend well to create a smooth batter. Dip desired food into batter and then coat with breadcrumbs. Deep fry at 350 degrees until golden brown. (good for fish, shrimp, seafood, or veggies)

SALMON CROQUETTES

Ingredients

2 cans Pink Salmon – 14.75 oz each

½ cp Contadina Traditional Breadcrumbs

1/8 cp All Purpose Flour

3 Eggs, Well Beaten

2 tsp Old Bay seasoning

1 tsp Cumin

2 tsp Onion Powder

1½ tsp Granulated Garlic

¼ tsp Ground Black Pepper

1 tbsp Lawry's Seasoned Salt

Coating Mix

1 cp Yellow Corn Meal

½ cp All Purpose Flour

1 Egg

1/8 cp Milk

Olive Oil

Directions

Prepare salmon for mixing by place one can at a time in a small bowl, using a fork look for and remove any bones, after this done place salmon in a large mixing bowl, add dry ingredient, and finally the eggs, mix well, shape the salmon into patties. For the coating, mix the egg and milk in a small bowl and beat, in a separate bowl mix the corn meal and flour, brush the patties with the milk and egg mixture, then cover with the coating mix, place the patties on a foil lined pan that has been coated with olive oil and then spray the top of the patties with olive oil and bake in a 425 degree pre-heated oven for 20 to 25 minutes or until patties are firm to the touch.

Variation

Fry patties in a small amount of olive oil 4 to 5 minutes per side or until brown.

Oven Fried Green Tomatoes, use Corn Meal Breading Mix, Page 12

GINGER SNAP VEGETABLE MEDLEY

Ingredients

8 oz - Sliced Carrots

8 oz – Broccoli Florets

8 oz – Cauliflower Florets

8 oz Sugar Snap Peas (with the strings removed)

8 oz Canned Baby Corn

Directions

Steam Carrots for 5 minutes, then add Sugar Snap peas and continue to steam for 5 more minutes. Add Broccoli, Cauliflower, and Baby Corn and continue to steam for 6 more minutes. Remove from heat and immediately add Ginger Butter Sauce. Serve hot.

GLAZED CARROTS AND APPLES

Ingredients:

1 ½lb Large Carrots

1lb or 3-4 Apples (Yellow)

½ cp Lemon Juice

1cp Water

1cp Light Brown Sugar

¾cp Granulated Sugar

1 ½tsp Nutmeg

1 ½tsp Cinnamon

1tsp Vanilla

3tsp Cornstarch

Directions

1. Wash and peel carrots, sliced carrots ¼ inch (angle cut) then set aside.
2. Peel and slice apples into ¼ inch slices. As the apples are slice, place them in a bowl of cold water with a ½ cup of lemon juice to avoid discoloration.
3. In a separate Bowl, combine all dry ingredients and mix well.
4. Drain carrots and place them in a pot with one cup of water.
5. Place pot over medium-high heat and bring to a boil, reduce heat and add dry ingredients and mix well.
6. Simmer 10 to 15 minutes or until carrots are ¾ done, Add apples, mix well and continue to simmer until apples are done but firm. If a thinner sauce is desired, add more water.
7. Serve hot. For smaller batches, reduce quantities.

GREEN BEANS AND TOMATOES W/OKRA

Ingredients

2 Slices of thick sliced Bacon (sliced into strips)

1 lb Fresh Green Beans (snap off ends and then snap into halves)

1 lb Stewed Tomatoes

¼ cp chopped yellow onions

1 tsp minced Garlic

½ tbsp Lawry's Seasoned Salt

1/8 tsp Ground Black Pepper

1 tsp Paprika

8 oz Frozen Okra

Directions

Steam Green Beans for 10 minutes and immediately shock in cold water, drain and set aside.

In a large sauté pan sauté Bacon pieces (do not brown)

Add Garlic and quickly stir (do not allow to burn)

Add Okra

Add onions, tomatoes and seasonings

Simmer for 15 to 20 minutes until Green Beans are fork tender

Variation

Substitute 2- 14.5 oz cans of Green Beans for the fresh Green Beans (drained and added to the mixture last)

Substitute 1 tsp Onion Powder for chopped Onions

Green Beans, Tomato and Okra; see Page 20

COLLARD AND MUSTARD GREENS W/SMOKED TURKEY

Ingredients

2 Smoked Turkey Tails

1tsp Minced Garlic

1tbsp Lawry's Seasoned Salt

1tsp Onion Powder

2 lb Collard Greens

2 lb Mustard Greens

½ cp Chopped Green Onions

1tbsp Baking Soda

Directions

Remove any feathers from the smoked turkey tails, place in pot that greens will be coked in, cover with water add seasonings bring to a boil reduce heat to rapid simmer and cook for 1 hour, wash clean and chop collards, add to pot, add baking soda and cook for another hour. wash clean and chop mustards and add to pot after 2nd hour, add green onions, mix well and continue to simmer another hour. Serve hot. For smaller batches, reduce quantities.

BAKED MACARONI AND CHEESE

Ingredients

12 oz Macaroni

1tbsp Olive Oil

2tsp Salt

2 ½ cups Milk

2 eggs

1 tbsp Paprika

¼ tsp Ground Black Pepper

1 ½ tsp Salt

8oz. Colby Jack Cheese

8oz Mild Cheddar Cheese

6 slices American cheese

Directions

In a sauce pan of water add the 1 tbsp of Olive and the 2 tsps. of salt and bring to a boil, then add the 12 oz of Macaroni and cook for about 8 minutes stirring occasionally to avoid sticking and clumping of the Macaroni, drain and rinse in cold water.

Mix together milk, eggs, paprika, black pepper, and salt and set aside. In a buttered baking pan layer as follows half of the Macaroni add layer on cheddar cheese and place slice American cheese the other half of the macaroni the layer of Colby Jack cheese stir and Pour in the milk and egg mixture and Bake in a 350-degree oven uncovered for 45 minutes. For smaller batches, reduce quantities.

Baked Macaroni and Cheese; see Page 23

GINGER BUTTER SAUCE

Ingredients

1 cp Melted Butter

1 tbsp Ground Ginger

1 tsp Ground Garlic

1/8 tsp Ground White Pepper

¼ tsp Salt

Directions

Combine all ingredients and mix well.

Variations:

1. Substitute melted butter for 1 cp clarified butter
2. substitute melted butter for 1 cp I can't believe its not butter, and omit salt

MUSTARD SAUCE

Ingredients

½ cup French's Mustard

½ tsp Granulated Garlic

½ tsp Onion Powder

1tsp Lawry's Seasoned Salt

1/8 tsp Black Pepper

ISLAND SALMON WITH MANGO SALSA

Ingredients

8 oz Fresh Salmon Fillet

½ tsp Chili Powder

½ tsp Ground Cumin

¼ tsp Ground Ginger

1tbsp Water

½ tsp Minced Garlic

Fresh Ground Black Pepper To Taste

1tsp Olive Oil

Mango Salsa (listed below)

Cilantro to garnish

Directions

In a large bowl, mix chili powder, cumin, ginger and garlic. Dust the spices onto the salmon by placing salmon skin side up into spices. In a large sauté pan, heat olive oil over high heat until it just begins to smoke. Cook the salmon spiced side down for about 30-50 seconds, until crust forms. Turn salmon spice side up at water to encourage Steam and bring heat down to medium-high.

Cover salmon for 4 to 7 minutes, taking care not to overcook, then garnish with mango salsa and cilantro.

MANGO SALSA

Ingredients:

2 Freshly Squeezed Limes,

2 Large Mangoes, Cut Into ½ Inch Cubes

4 tsp Green Onions, Thinly Sliced

1 tbsp Jalapeno Peppers Minced

1 ½ tsp Honey

Freshly Ground Pepper and Sea Salt To Taste

½ cup cilantro coarsely chopped

Directions

In a medium bowl, combine all ingredients except cilantro. Let stand for 20 minutes to allow flavors to develop then add cilantro just before serving to allow flavors to develop. Then add cilantro just before serving

MASHED BUTTER PECAN SWEET POTATOES

Ingredients

1 ½ lbs Sweet Potatoes Peeled and Sliced

2 tbsp Butter

1 cp Light Brown Sugar

1 tsp Mace

1 cp Toasted Pecans (Chopped)

Directions

Place potatoes in a medium saucepan, cover with cold water, boil until tender. Drain off water, whip the potatoes, add butter, sugar, mace, and mix well. Add chopped pecans and serve hot.

CHICKEN & SHRIMP CORN CHOWDER

Ingredients

½ lb. Chicken Thighs

½ lb. Shrimp

½ cp Chopped Celery

½ cp Red or Orange Bell Pepper

1cp Celery Flakes

¼ tsp White Pepper

½ tbsp Lawry's Seasoned Salt

½ tsp Granulated Garlic

½ tsp Onion Powder

1 can Whole Kernel Corn

1 can Diced Potatoes

1 ½ cup Liquid (chicken stock and or liquid from vegetables)

2 cans of Campbell's Cream of Chicken Soup

Directions

Bake chicken, seasoned with garlic, onion powder, black pepper and Lawry's Seasoned salt. Let cool and chop into cubes

Sauté shrimp in a small amount of olive oil shrimp can be kept whole or chopped

In a saucepan, combine soup and liquid and ingredients, bring to a boil, reduce heat and simmer for 20 minutes

Serving suggestion: serve over a warm biscuit

SAVORY SMOTHERED CABBAGE

Ingredients

1 Small Cabbage (Quartered and Cored)

3 Slices Thick Slice Bacon (Cut into Strips)

½ Red Bell Pepper (Cut into Strips)

½ cp Chopped Green Onions

1 cp Water

1 tbsp Lawry's Seasoned Salt

Directions

Sauté bacon in a large sauté pan that has a lid or a Dutch oven over high heat, do not overcook. Reduce heat, add peppers, and cabbage and cook for 10 minutes. Add remaining ingredients and bring to a boil. Reduce heat and continue to cook over a medium heat for about 20 minutes, stirring occasionally until cabbage is tender.

HONEY MUSTARD CORNISH HENS

Ingredients

2 Rock Cornish Hens

½ tbsp Granulated Garlic

½ tbsp Onion Powder

¼ tsp Ground Black Pepper

½ tbsp Lawry's Seasoned Salt

1 tbsp Ground Mustard

½ cp Honey

Directions

Pre heat oven to 350 degrees

Mix together all dry ingredients. Rinse and dry Hens and then brush with the Honey. Sprinkle with dry ingredients and place in a small roasting pan and cover and Bake for 30 minutes, uncover and continue to bake for another 30 minutes or until golden brown and Hens reach an internal temperature of 160 degrees.

CHICKEN AND SHRIMP JAMBALAYA

Ingredients

6 cps Water

3 tbsp Tone's Chicken Base (other brands may be too salty and less should be used)

1 tsp Dried Thyme Leaves

1 tsp Dried Basil Leaves

1 tsp Ground Ginger

1 tsp Granulated Garlic

½ cp Orange Bell Pepper

¼ cp Chopped Onion

½ cp Chopped Celery

½ cp Chopped Portobello Mushrooms

2 tbsp Olive Oil

1 lb. Fresh Chicken Breast Cut into Strips

1 lb. Peeled and Deveined Shrimp Sliced Crosswise

1 cp Water

5 tbsp Corn Starch

4 cp Cooked White Rice

Directions:

In a large saucepan bring water to a boil, add chicken base and stir until dissolved, add thyme, basil, ginger, and garlic, reduce and simmer for 25 minutes. Prepare rice and add to the pot, in a small bowl mix the 1 cp water and corn starch, pour mixture slowly into pot while it simmers, 4 to 5 minutes until liquid thickens. Serve hot.

5-DAY MARINADE

Ingredients

½ cp Brown sugar

½ cp Soy Sauce

½ cp Lemon Juice

½ tbsp Onion Powder

½ tbsp Granulated Garlic

¼ tsp Black Pepper

½ tbsp ground Cumin

1 tsp basil leaves

1 to 2 Apples sliced and added to mixture

1 to 2 oranges quartered squeeze the juice in and add oranges

Directions

Combine all ingredients in large pot add desired meat cover with water, marinade up to 5 days, drain or retain liquid, pat meat dry, brush with olive oil and cook using your desired method. Smoke, grill, bake, broil, and or fry. For smaller batches, reduce quantities.

Smoked Duck after 5-Day Marinade, Page 36

SPAGHETTI SAUCE

Ingredients

2 cans Stewed Tomatoes (drain and retain liquid)

1 can Mushroom Stems and Pieces (drain and retain liquid)

1 15 oz can Tomato Sauce

2 6 oz cans tomato paste

4 ½ cp Liquid (use liquid from stewed tomatoes and mushrooms the rest water)

1 tbsp Granulated Garlic

2 tsp Onion Powder

¼ tsp Ground Black Pepper

1 ½ tbsp Dried Oregano Flakes

1 ½ tsp Dried Basil Leaves

½ tsp Dried Thyme

- Combine all ingredients in large pot, add desired meat and cover with water

2 tbsp Paprika

2 tsp Salt

2 tbsp Granulated Sugar

Directions

Bring liquids to a simmer and add dry ingredients one at a time stirring well after each addition, and then add mushrooms and tomatoes continue to simmer another 20 minutes.

Variation

Add 1lb browned and drained ground beef and ½ lb sliced cooked Italian sausage to make Meat Sauce.

For Pizza Sauce, add additional 1tbsp Sugar. For smaller batches, reduce quantities.

LISHA'S LEMON GARLIC BUTTER SAUCE FOR SEAFOOD

Ingredients

Use whole milk or cream with water. Do not use low-fat milk or the sauce may curdle.

1/2 cup clam juice (can substitute chicken stock)

1/2 cup dry sherry

1/2 cup whole milk
(OR 3 Tbsp cream with 5 Tbsp water)

1 Tbsp minced garlic

1 Tbsp minced shallots

1 bay leaf

1 Tbsp unsalted butter

1 1/2 Tbsp flour

1/2 pound (2 sticks) unsalted butter

1/2 teaspoon salt

1/2 teaspoon white pepper

1 Tbsp lemon juice

Directions:

Simmer and reduce the liquids, with garlic, shallots, and bay leaf: Place first six ingredients (clam juice, sherry, whole milk, garlic, shallots, bay leaf) in a small saucepan. Heat on medium high heat and let simmer until the liquids have reduced by about half. Make a roux: In a separate saucepan (1-qt minimum) prepare the roux. Heat one tablespoon of butter in the saucepan on medium heat until it is foamy. Sprinkle in the flour, stirring a couple of minutes with a metal whisk until well mixed (tan, but not browned).

Slowly add liquid mixture to roux: Slowly add the reduced mixture to the roux, stirring quickly to incorporate. When you first add some of the mixture, the roux will bubble up. Just keep adding the mixture and keep whisking to incorporate.

Slowly incorporate butter, 2 Tbsp at a time: Lower the heat to low. Remove the bay leaf. Slowly whisk in the butter, 2 tablespoons at a time. Let the butter tablespoons fully melt and be incorporated into the sauce before adding more tablespoons.

Stir in lemon juice, salt, and white pepper. Add some more clam stock or water if the sauce is too thick. Add cluster of shredded crab legs, a cup of chopped shrimp and mushrooms(personal preference for amount)

STIR FRY

Ingredients

8 oz Carrots (peeled and sliced)

4 oz Red, Yellow or Orange Bell Pepper (strips)

2 oz Fresh Water Crest Leaves

4 oz Water Crest Stalks (sliced)

5 oz Water Chestnuts (sliced) retain the liquid

4 oz Baby Corn (retain the liquid)

4 oz Portobello Mushrooms (sliced)

1 lb. Chicken Breast (cut into strips)

1 lb. Shrimp

3 tsp Ground Ginger

2 tsp Onion Powder

1 tsp Granulated Garlic

1 ½ tsp Lawry's Seasoned Salt

2 tbsp Soy Sauce

2 tsp Cornstarch

½ cp Reserved Liquid

2 tbsp Olive Oil

Directions

Gather all ingredients, heat wok or large sauté pan, add olive oil, add in the following order, carrots, chicken strips, water chestnuts, water crest stalks, bell pepper, baby corn, mushrooms, water crest leaves, shrimp, soy sauce and dry ingredients.

In a small bowl or cup mix reserve liquid and corn starch, pour into mixture while stirring and heat for another 2 to 3 minutes, remove from heat and serve over steamed rice.

Variation

Substitute or add your favorite vegetables or meats

LINDA'S UPSIDE- DOWN TURKEY

Items needed

1 - 15 to 20 lb. turkey completely thawed

1 box Reynolds oven roasting bags for turkey size 20lb or larger large roasting pan to accommodate the size of turkey you have

Ingredients

Accent Meat Tenderizer

Lawry's Seasoned Salt

Garlic Powder

Poultry Seasoning (optional)

2 tbsp Flour

1 Large Onion

6 stalks of celery

2 large oranges (optional)

Directions

Buford Family Favorites

Preheat oven 15 minutes at 350 degrees

Remove all additional turkey parts from the inside of the turkey (turkey neck gizzards and liver). Rinse wash turkey in cold water. Dry completely the inside and outside of the turkey.

Using a clean area to season the turkey, begin by using your oranges. Rub oranges on table to loosen up the juices, sliced in half and rub orange all over the turkey inside and out. Place oranges aside once you are finished rubbing down the turkey. Season inside and outside liberally with accent, garlic powder, Lawry's Seasoned salt, and (poultry seasoning if using). Use the same seasonings on the additional turkey Parts as well.

Take your oven roasting bag and place it inside your roasting pan and do the following steps: Open the bag and sprinkle the two tbsp of flour in the bag. Slice the onion into 6-8 slices, place the slices on top of the flour in the bag. Cut each celery stalk into two pieces, place the six pieces in the bag on and around the onion slices. Take turkey and place it breast side down inside the oven roasting bag. Place the remaining celery onion and if you use oranges, place those as well into the cavity of the turkey. Place additional turkey parts in the bag. Close the bag with the twist tie. Make 7 1-inch slits in the top of the oven roasting bag to release the steam. Do not open the bag at any time during the cooking process. Cook your turkey at 350 degrees for 30 minutes per pound. For smaller batches, reduce quantities.

LINDA'S GRAVY

To make gravy for turkey or roasting hen, you should use any juices you may have from the turkey or hen. Taste the juices to make sure it's not salty, add some water to dilute. If you do not have any juices remaining you may use chicken broth.

Ingredients

1/3 cp vegetable oil

2/3 cp flour

½ tsp accent meat tenderizer

½ tsp garlic powder

½ tsp Lawry's Seasoned salt

¼ tsp garlic salt

2/3 cp finely chopped onion

2/3 cp finely chopped green pepper

Gravy Master for Browning (you can find this item in the sauces or gravy section in your grocery store)

2-4 cups hot liquid water, juices from your cooked turkey or hen or chicken broth, add more water or broth if needed.

Directions

Place oil in a Skillet or stainless-steel pot and let it get hot over medium Heat (do not burn. If you burn the oil you must start over close parentheses. A flour gradually, until you create a thin paste. Continuous stirring is needed to keep the pace nice and smooth. Add seasonings, onions and green peppers. Continue cooking until the paste starts to Brown lightly (do not burn) to the color consistency you want without burning. Add liquid to the paced mixture and continue stirring. Your mixture may require more or less liquid as it continues to cook. Taste the gravy, add more seasoning if necessary. If your gravy isn't the right color you want, gradually add the Gravy Master to add a richer, darker color to the gravy.

Gravy thickening agent use only if gravy needs to be thickened 2 tbsp cornstarch mixed with cold water to make a medium to thin paste. For smaller batches, reduce quantities.

CAROLYN'S CORNBREAD DRESSING

Ingredients

4cups Cornbread

½ Loaf White Bread

½ Loaf Wheal Bread

1 ½ lb. Turkey Necks (Fresh Or Raw)

1lb Chicken Gizzards

1 cup Celery

¼ cup Green Onion

1 cup Green Bell Pepper

1 tbsp Poultry Seasoning

1 tbsp Sage

4oz or ½ Stick Melted Butter

4 Hard Boiled Eggs

1 tsp Granulated Garlic

1 tbsp Lawry's Seasoned Salt

56oz or 7 cp Chicken Stock

Directions
- Cook turkey necks (if using fresh, fully cook and debone) (liquid can be retained to be used in place of chicken stock. If using smoked turkey debone and chop
- Fully cook chicken gizzards and chop. liquid may be retained to be used in place of chicken stock.
- Make cornbread and toast and dice breads.
- Chop celery and onions and hard-boiled eggs
- Combine all ingredients. Mixture should be a little loose but not too watery. Add additional bread or stock as needed.
- Cook at 350 degrees covered for 45 minutes continue to cook uncovered until firm to the touch. For smaller batches, reduce quantities.

BAR-B-QUE SPARE RIBS

Directions

Trim the fat and remove the membrane from the back of 2 slabs of Pork ribs, cut off the tips and cut into pieces, rinse and place in a stock pot, add multi- purpose marinade and cover with water and refrigerate for 24 to 48 hour for best results. Remove from refrigerator and Discard marinade rinse meat and pat dry, brush with olive and and lightly season with Lawry's season salt, let stand for 1 hour and grill or smoke until done.

Variation:

Substitute: pork ribs with beef ribs or chicken, do not par-boil chicken, place directly onto hot grill

Smoked Rib Tips after Marinading in Multi-Purpose Marinade, Page 5

CHILLI

Ingredients

2 cans Red Kidney Beans

1 ½ lb. Ground Beef

½ cup Chopped Onion

½ cup Red Bell Pepper

1 can Stewed Tomato

4 tbsp Chili Powder

3 tbsp Cumin

2 tbsp Paprika

2 tsp Basil Leaves

2 tsp Thyme

Directions:

In a large skillet, Brown, drain and set aside ground beef. in a medium saucepan, Place kidney beans tomato and dry ingredients, mix well and add ground beef simmer for 20 minutes. For smaller batches, reduce quantities.

CHICKEN POT PIE

Ingredients

1 ½ lb. Skinless Chicken Thighs

1 can Sliced Carrots

1can Whole Kernel Corn

1 can Green Beans

1 can Diced Potatoes

1 can Lima Beans

1 can Mushrooms (optional)

1 can Cream of Chicken Soup

1 tbsp of Lawry's Seasoned Salt

1 tsp Black Pepper Ground

1 tsp Granulated Garlic

1 tsp Onion Powder

2 ½ cup liquid (chicken stock or reserve liquid from vegetables)

1 Egg

Pie Crust on page 58; double the recipe

Season chicken as you like Bake and chop chicken thighs in a large mixing bowl, combine all ingredients. Roll out bottom layer of pie crust. Place crust in aluminum half pan. Add mixture and top crust, cramp sides. Brush top of crust with well beaten egg and make perforation in the crust to allow steam to escape. Bake at 425 degrees for 20 minutes, lower heat to 350 degrees and continue bake until crust is golden brown or 45 minutes. For smaller batches, reduce quantities.

Variation: substitute chicken with turkey or pork or use canned chunk chicken

Peach Cobbler, Page 58

RAYMOND'S SALMON WITH LEMON BUTTER CAPERS

Ingredients

Ingredients
2-4, 6 oz portions of King Salmon (Chinook), with skin on, scaled (Or use more readily available Wild Caught Atlantic Salmon. For an even better taste use smoked salmon; or smoke it yourself on the grill. Do not use Sockeye Salmon, as the taste is too overbearing).

4 oz White wine
(Can be substituted with 2 Tbs of white vinegar diluted with water to make 4 oz).

10 oz Chopped Shallots
(Or substitute green onions-- very colorful)

2 oz Drained Capers

2 oz Lemon Juice

6 oz Soft butter (If bothered by dairy, substitute with Nucoa instead).

Directions:

1. Lightly flour salmon and pan sear in a little oil until browned. Remove from pan and place in shallow Pyrex dish and bake at 350° for 10 min or until salmon is firm.
2. Sauce: Combine wine, shallots, and capers in a fry pan. Sauté over medium heat. Reduce by ½.
3. Add: lemon juice and remove from heat. Add butter bit by bit, rolling the pan to melt butter, without breaking it down into oil.
4. Plate salmon and spoon sauce liberally over salmon.
5. Serve with favorite rice dish or petite red potatoes and vegetables

PIE CRUST

Ingredients

2cp all-purpose flour

1 tsp salt

1 tbsp granulated sugar

2/3 cp Crisco shortening

8 tbsp cold water

Directions

Mix together dry ingredients, cut in shortening until mixture is crumbly, add water and mix until dough is formed, do not over mix, and let rest before rolling.

Sweet Potato Pie; see Page 57

SWEET POTATO PIE (FILLING)

Ingredients

2 lb. Small Sweet Potatoes

1 cp Eagle Brand Fat Free Sweetened Condensed Milk

1 cp Light Brown Sugar

2/3 cp Granulated Sugar

3 Well Beaten Eggs

1 tsp Cinnamon

1tsp Mace

1 tsp Vanilla Extract

Directions

Peel and slice sweet potatoes, place in a medium saucepan and cover with cold water, bring to a boil and cook until potatoes are tender and can be mashed with a fork. Drain and place hot in food processor add milk, sugars, and spices, puree then slowly fold in volumized eggs by whipping eggs vigorously with a wire whip in a small bowl to incorporate air into the eggs a wand can also be used, pour mixture into pie crust (page 57) lined pie pans, bake in a 425 degree oven for 15 minutes reduce heat to 350 degrees and continue to bake for 45 minutes until pie bellows remove pies and let cool can be served warm or cold. Makes 2 pies.

PEACH COBBLER

Ingredients

1 #10 can Peaches (drained)

1 cp Light Brown Sugar

1 ½ cp Granulated Sugar

2 tsp Ground Nutmeg

1 ¼ tsp Ground Cinnamon

4 tbsp Corn Starch

2 tsp Vanilla Extract

1 Egg (room temperature and well beaten)

Buford Family Favorites

Extra granulated sugar to sprinkled on top of prepare pie

Crust

4 cps All Purpose Flour

2 tsp Salt

3 tbsp Granulated Sugar

1 ½ cp Crisco Shortening

1 cp Ice Cold Water

Directions

Place drained peaches in a large mixing bowl, in a separate bowl mix all dry ingredients and mix well with a fork, pour dry mixture over the peaches mix and refrigerate for at least 30 minutes but overnight is best

For the crust, mix together dry ingredients add shortening and mix by hand until mixture has a crumbly texture, add water and mix just until all ingredient comes together to form a dough do not over mix, let the dough rest for 20 minutes. Roll out¾ of the dough and place in your steamtable half pan pour in peach mixture and top with pie crust, braid or crimp the edges and, brush with beaten egg, sprinkle on granulated sugar and make some piercings in the crust to allow steam to escape while pie cooking. Bake at 425 degrees for 20 minutes reduce heat to 350 degrees and bake about 1 huor until golden brown, let cool can be served hot or cold

LOUISIANA STYLE SEAFOOD GUMBO

Rouge Ingredients

2cps All Purpose Flour

2cps Olive Oil

1tbsp Kitchen Bouquet

Gumbo Ingredients

2lbs Chicken Gizzards

2lbs Eckrich Beef Sausage

4lbs Chicken Wingettes

2lbs Fresh Shrimp

4lbs Crab Claws (Fresh or Frozen)

1-2oz Package Dried Shrimp

1cp. Chopped Celery

2cp Chopped Onions

Buford Family Favorites

2cp Chopped Green Bell Pepper

2-15oz Cans Diced Tomatoes

2-15oz Cans Cut Baby Corn

12 oz Frozen Cut Okra

1 Sprig Fresh Thyme

3 Sprigs Fresh Rosemary

2 Sprigs Fresh Oregano

4 Leaves Fresh Bay Leaves

3 Leaves Fresh Basil

6qt Chicken Stock

3tbsp Granulated Garlic

1tsp Ground Black Pepper

4tbsp Old Bay Seasoning

6tbsp Lawry's Seasoned Salt

2tbsp Gumbo File

1cp Worchestershire Sauce

2 Cheese Cloths

Preparation
- Boil chicken gizzards until done. Strain and reserve liquid
- Boil chicken wingettes until ¾ done. Strain and reserve liquid
- Cut fresh shrimp into bite size pieces (leave raw). Place to side
- Chop celery, onion and bell peppers
- Place herbs into a piece of cheese cloth and tie
- Place dried shrimp into a separate piece of cheese cloth and tie

Directions
Heat olive oil in a skillet (cast iron is best). Slowly add flour and stir constantly until the rouge is the color is the color of milk chocolate (do not burn). This process will take about 20 minutes. Put rouge into large stock pot over low heat. Add Kitchen Bouquet and Worchestershire Sauce and mix well. Add vegetables (except Okra) and sweat until done (onions will be clear). Add 6 quarts of stock (reserve liquids can be used to make up the 6 quarts). Add herbs and dried shrimp in their cheese cloths (will be removed after Gumbo is completely cooked). Add gizzards, chicken drummettes and sausage and simmer for about 20 minutes. Add raw shrimp and crab claws.

Add granulated garlic, black pepper, Old Bay and Lawry's Seasoned Salt and mix well. Add Gumbo File and mix well (sauce will thicken). Turn off heat, add Okra and mix well. Cover the pot and let the Gumbo set (Okra will cook enough while pot is off without falling apart). Remove both cheese cloth packages. Serve over rice.

Variation: for smaller batches, decrease ingredients, except dried shrimp and herbs